THE ORIGINAL SHOOTERS GUIDE
by Cindy Campbell

Published by Bookwork Productions Ltd.
Edmonton, Alberta, Canada
Second Printing — 1985
Copyright © 1985

ISBN 0-9692284-0-6

ACKNOWLEDGEMENTS

I WOULD LIKE TO EXTEND SPECIAL THANKS TO CHRIS KYRIACOU FROM "SHOOTERS DINE AND DANCE" FOR PERMITTING ME TO USE HIS RECIPES IN MY BOOK. "SHOOTERS DINE AND DANCE" IS ONE OF THE ORIGINAL SHOOTERS BARS IN EDMONTON AND CHRIS KEEPS THE PRICES LOW ENOUGH SO THAT YOU CAN AFFORD TO TRY AS MANY OF HIS SHOOTERS AS YOU CAN HANDLE.

TABLE OF CONTENTS

INTRODUCTION

THE SHOOTER - A GREAT NEW WAY OF ENJOYING LIQUEURS. DEMANDING A STEADY HAND THE LIQUEURS ARE CAREFULLY LAYERED ONE ON TOP OF THE OTHER ONLY TO BE SHOT BACK IN ONE SWIFT SMOOTH MOTION.

SHOOTERS ARE A FAIRLY NEW TRADITION AND THUS ONLY A FEW POPULAR MIXTURES ARE UNIVERSALLY KNOWN UNDER THE SAME NAME. SOME OF THESE BEING JELLY BEANS, B-52'S AND UPSIDE DOWN MARGARITAS.

IN RESEARCHING MATERIAL FOR THIS BOOK I CAME ACROSS SEVERAL COMBINATIONS OF LIQUEURS WITH MANY DIFFERENT NAMES. IT SOON BECAME CLEAR THAT MOST BARTENDERS SIMPLY MAKE UP THEIR OWN CONCOCTIONS AND CREATE THEIR OWN NAMES. TAKING THIS INTO CONSIDERATION ONE MAY WANT TO INQUIRE ABOUT THE INGREDIENTS USED WHEN ORDERING A SPECIFIC SHOOTER.

THE FOLLOWING RECIPES HAVE BEEN COMPILED FROM A VARIETY OF SOURCES. "SHOOTERS DINE AND DANCE" PROVIDED QUITE A LARGE NUMBER. OTHERS WERE GIVEN TO ME FROM FRIENDS AND THEN OF COURSE I CREATED SOME OF MY OWN.

DON'T BE AFRAID TO EXPERIMENT AND CREATE YOUR OWN SHOOTERS. THE ONLY PROBLEM YOU MAY HAVE IS FINDING LIQUEURS WHICH WILL LAYER NICELY. IF THE LAYERS RUN TOGETHER AND YOU CREATE A MILKY MESS, SIMPLY INFORM YOUR GUESTS THAT YOU ARE SERVING A " MUD SLINGER".

TOOLS OF THE TRADE

GLASSES:

SHOOTER GLASSES, OR

SHOT GLASSES, OR

$1\frac{1}{2}$ – 2 oz. LIQUEUR GLASSES.

BEGINNERS BAR:

THE FIVE MOST POPULAR SHOOTER INGREDIENTS ARE LISTED BELOW. I WOULD START OFF WITH THESE AND GRADUALLY ADD TO YOUR BAR.

KAHLUA

IRISH CREAM

CREME DE BANANES

GRAND MARNIER

TEQUILA

A GREAT WAY TO STOCK YOUR BAR IS TO HAVE A SHOOTERS PARTY AND ASK THAT EACH GUEST BRING A DIFFERENT LIQUEUR.

POURING TECHNIQUES

THE SKILL OF LAYERING LIQUEURS CAN ONLY BE MASTERED AFTER HOURS OF PRACTICE. THE EXPERTS IN THE FIELD USE NOTHING MORE THAN A STEADY HAND. AMATEURS, HOWEVER, OFTEN PREFER TO USE A TEASPOON HELD UPSIDE DOWN AGAINST THE INSIDE OF THE GLASS. THE LIQUEUR IS POURED ON THE ROUND OF THE SPOON THEN IT GENTLY FLOWS DOWN THE SIDE OF THE GLASS AND SETTLES ON TOP OF THE PREVIOUS LIQUEUR. THE THIRD LIQUEUR IS OFTEN POURED SO THAT IT FLOWS THROUGH THE SECOND LIQUEUR AND RESTS ON TOP OF THE FIRST.

SUBSTITUTIONS

 THESE SUBSTITUTIONS APPLY ONLY TO THE FLAVORS. THEY MAY NOT HAVE THE SAME DENSITY AND THUS MIGHT NOT LAYER PROPERLY.

COFFEE LIQUEURS:

 CAFE ROYAL

 ESPANOLA SPANISH

 KAHLUA

 CAFE DE PARIS

 ALOHA

 TIA MARIA

CREAM LIQUEURS:

 BAILEY'S IRISH

 CAROLAN'S IRISH

 KEMPER'S BAVARIAN

 O'DARBY DAIRY IRISH

ORANGE LIQUEURS: COINTREAU

GRAND CURACAO

GRAND MARNIER

TAMARIND

TANGO BRANDY & MANDARINE

TRIPLE SEC

ANISE (BLACK LICORICE):   ANISETTE

LIQUORE D'ORO

OUZO

SAMBUCA

TOP TEN

AFTER EIGHT

B - 52

BANANA SPLIT

BLOW JOB

EH - BOMB

EL REVOLTO

HEAVENLY BODY

JELLY BEAN

NUDE BOMB

ZUC

GLOSSARY

LIQUEURS

LIQUEURS ARE ALCOHOLIC BEVERAGES PREPARED THROUGH THE PROCESS OF IN-FUSION, PERCOLATION OR DISTILLATION. MADE FROM COMPLEX FORMULAS CONTAINING A BASE OF BRANDY OR OTHER SPIRITS, SUGAR OR SYRUP, AND FLAVORINGS FROM FRUITS, FLOWERS, HERBS, SEEDS, SPICES, ROOTS, BARK OR KERNALS FROM AROUND THE WORLD.

THE ALCOHOL CONTENT OF LIQUEURS CAN VARY BUT THE MINIMUM ALLOWED IS 23%. THE HIGHER THE ALCOHOL CONTENT, THE LONGER THE SHELF LIFE. AFTER A LENGTHY PERIOD ON THE SHELF A LIQUEUR WOULD NOT GENERALLY TURN SOUR OR BECOME A DRINKING HAZARD BUT THE FLAVOR MAY BEGIN TO DETERIORATE. CREAM LIQUEURS ARE MORE PERISHABLE THAN OTHER LIQUEURS AND THEREFORE SHOULD BE REFRIGERATED AFTER OPENING. FOR OPTIMUM QUALITY IT IS RECOMMENDED THAT CREAM LIQUEURS BE CONSUMED WITHEN SIX MONTHS AFTER PURCHASE.

ALOHA

COUNTRY OF ORIGIN: CANADA

ALCOHOL %: 25.0

SHELF LIFE: INDEFINITE

STORAGE: STORE UPRIGHT IN A
COOL DARK AREA.

CHARACTERISTICS: DARK BROWN IN COLOUR, RICH COFFEE FLAVOUR.

****

ADVOCAAT

COUNTRY OF ORIGIN: HOLLAND

ALCOHOL %: 15.0

SHELF LIFE: 2 YEARS

STORAGE: STORE UPRIGHT IN A
COOL DARK AREA.

CHARACTERISTICS: A BLEND OF EGG YOLKS, SUGAR, AROMATIC SPIRITS
AND BRANDEWIJN.

AMERELLO

COUNTRY OF ORIGIN: CANADA

ALCOHOL %: 17.0

SHELF LIFE: INDEFINITE

STORAGE: REFRIGERATE AFTER
OPENING

CHARACTERISTICS: COMBINES THE TASTE OF AMARETTO WITH FRESH DAIRY CREAM
AND GRACEFULLY AGED SPIRITS.

****

AMARETTO

COUNTRY OF ORIGIN: CANADA

ALCOHOL %: 28.0

SHELF LIFE: INDEFINITE

STORAGE: STORE UPRIGHT IN A
COOL DARK AREA.

CHARACTERISTICS: MEDIUM BROWN IN COLOUR, RICH AMARETTO-NUT FLAVOUR.

ANISETTE

COUNTRY OF ORIGIN: CANADA

ALCOHOL %: 25.0

SHELF LIFE: 1 YEAR

STORAGE: STORE UPRIGHT IN A
COOL DARK AREA.

CHARACTERISTICS: A BLEND OF NATURAL FLAVOUR, SUGAR AND GRAIN SPIRITS.
COLOURLESS, ANISE FLAVOUR

****

APRICOT BRANDY

COUNTRY OF ORIGIN: CANADA

ALCOHOL %: 25.0

SHELF LIFE: INDEFINITE

STORAGE: STORE UPRIGHT IN A
COOL DARK AREA.

CHARACTERISTICS: SWEET APRICOT AND BRANDY FLAVOUR.

B & B (BENEDICTINE & BRANDY)

COUNTRY OF ORIGIN: FRANCE

ALCOHOL %: 40.0

SHELF LIFE: INDEFINITE

STORAGE: STORE UPRIGHT IN A
          COOL DARK AREA.

CHARACTERISTICS: MIXTURE OF BENEDICTINE – (27 DIFFERENT PLANTS HERBS AND
                 SPICES DISTILLED, STEEPED AND INFUSED) AND OLD COGNAC.

****

BAILEY'S ORIGINAL IRISH CREAM

COUNTRY OF ORIGIN: IRELAND

ALCOHOL %: 17.0

SHELF LIFE: 1 YEAR

STORAGE: REFRIGERATE
          AFTER OPENING

CHARACTERISTICS: A BLEND OF FRESH CREAM AND IRISH WHISKEY WITH
                  CHOCOLATE NOTES.

BENEDICTINE (D.O.M.)

COUNTRY OF ORIGIN: FRANCE

ALCOHOL %: 40.0

SHELF LIFE: INDEFINITE

STORAGE: STORE UPRIGHT IN A
COOL DARK AREA.

CHARACTERISTICS: MADE FROM 27 DIFFERENT PLANTS, HERBS AND SPICES
DISTILLED,STEEPED AND INFUSED. ALLOWED TO BECOME
OLD BEFORE MIXING WITH BASIC ALCOHOLS.

****

BLACKBERRY BRANDY

COUNTRY OF ORIGIN: CANADA

ALCOHOL %: 25.0

SHELF LIFE: INDEFINITE

STORAGE: STORE UPRIGHT IN A
COOL DARK AREA.

CHARACTERISTICS: DARK RED BLACKBERRY COLOUR AND FLAVOUR.

CASSIS - BLACK CURRANT

COUNTRY OF ORIGIN: HOLLAND   SHELF LIFE: 1 YEAR

ALCOHOL %: 23.0   STORAGE: STORE UPRIGHT IN A

        COOL DARK AREA.

CHARACTERISTICS: BASED ON BLACKCURRANT EXTRACT WITH NATURAL AND
NATURE-IDENTICAL FRUIT-FLAVOURS.

****

BLUE CURACAO

COUNTRY OF ORIGIN: HOLLAND   SHELF LIFE: INDEFINITE

ALCOHOL %: 34.0   STORAGE: STORE UPRIGHT IN A

        COOL DARK AREA.

CHARACTERISTICS: MADE FROM THE PEEL OF SMALL GREEN ORANGES, SPICES AND
SOMETIMES PORT WINE OR RUM.

BERENTZEN APPEL

COUNTRY OF ORIGIN: WEST GERMANY SHELF LIFE: INDEFINITE

ALCOHOL %: 25.0 STORAGE: STORE UPRIGHT IN A
COOL DARK AREA.

CHARACTERISTICS: AMBER COLOUR WITH A TYPICAL ODOUR AND
FLAVOUR OF APPLE.

****

CAFE DE PARIS

COUNTRY OF ORIGIN: CANADA SHELF LIFE: 2 YEARS

ALCOHOL %: 25.0 STORAGE: STORE UPRIGHT IN A
COOL DARK AREA.

CHARACTERISTICS: RICH BROWN LIQUEUR WITH DISTINCTIVE TASTE OF COFFEE.

CAFE ROYAL

COUNTRY OF ORIGIN: CANADA

ALCOHOL %: 25.0

SHELF LIFE: INDEFINITE

STORAGE: STORE UPRIGHT IN A
COOL DARK AREA.

CHARACTERISTICS: BLACK COFFEE COLOUR, WITH COFFEE FLAVOUR.

****

COGNAC

COUNTRY OF ORIGIN: FRANCE

ALCOHOL %: 40.0 %

SHELF LIFE: INDEFINITE

STORAGE: STORE UPRIGHT IN A
COOL DARK AREA.

CHARACTERISTICS: THE FINEST OF BRANDIES MADE FROM GRAPES GROWN AROUND
THE FRENCH CITY OF COGNAC.

CAMPARI

COUNTRY OF ORIGIN: CANADA

ALCOHOL %: 25.0

SHELF LIFE: INDEFINITE

STORAGE: STORE UPRIGHT IN A
COOL DARK AREA.

CHARACTERISTICS: AN APPETIZER DERIVED FROM AN INFUSION OF AROMATIC AND
BITTER HERBS AND ORANGE PEELS. RUBY-RED IN COLOUR.

****

CAROLAN'S IRISH CREAM

COUNTRY OF ORIGIN: IRELAND

ALCOHOL %: 17.0

SHELF LIFE: 1 YEAR

STORAGE: REFRIGERATE
AFTER OPENING

CHARACTERISTICS: A BLEND OF CREAM, WHISKEY, NEUTRAL SPIRIT, HONEY,
SUGAR AND STEARYL-LACTYLATE.

CHARTREUSE

COUNTRY OF ORIGIN: FRANCE   SHELF LIFE: INDEFINITE

ALCOHOL %: 40.0   STORAGE: STORE UPRIGHT IN A

                                                   COOL DARK AREA.

CHARACTERISTICS: BELIEVED TO BE MADE OF SOME 130 HERBS, IT HAS BEEN MADE

                  BY CARTHUSIAN MONKS SINCE 1605.

****

CHERRY BRANDY

COUNTRY OF ORIGIN: CANADA   SHELF LIFE: INDEFINITE

ALCOHOL %: 25.0   STORAGE: STORE UPRIGHT IN A

                                                   COOL DARK AREA.

CHARACTERISTICS: RED COLOUR WITH A SWEET CHERRY BRANDY FLAVOUR.

CHERRY WHISKEY

COUNTRY OF ORIGIN: CANADA

ALCOHOL %: 25.0

SHELF LIFE: 2 YEARS

STORAGE: STORE UPRIGHT IN A
COOL DARK AREA.

CHARACTERISTICS: PRODUCED FROM A BLEND OF WHISKEY, ALCOHOL, FRUIT
JUICE AND NATURAL CHERRY FLAVOURS.

****

CHESTNUT LIQUEUR

COUNTRY OF ORIGIN: CANADA

ALCOHOL %: 25.0

SHELF LIFE: INDEFINITE

STORAGE: STORE UPRIGHT IN A
COOL DARK AREA.

CHARACTERISTICS: ASSORTED CHESTNUT FLAVOURS, GRAIN, NEUTRAL SPIRITS
AND GRAPE BRANDY.

CHOCOLATE ALMOND

COUNTRY OF ORIGIN: CANADA

ALCOHOL %: 25.0

SHELF LIFE: 2 YEARS

STORAGE: STORE UPRIGHT IN A
COOL DARK AREA.

CHARACTERISTICS: A SWEET LIQUEUR WHICH IS A BLEND OF COCOA, CHOCOLATE
AND ALMOND FLAVOUR.

****

CHU YEN CHING

COUNTRY OF ORIGIN: CHINA

ALCOHOL %: 47.0

SHELF LIFE: INDEFINITE

STORAGE: STORE UPRIGHT IN A
COOL DARK AREA.

CHARACTERISTICS: A LIGHT YELLOW COLOURED LIQUEUR WITH A
FRAGRANT NOSE.

COINTREAU

COUNTRY OF ORIGIN: FRANCE

ALCOHOL %: 40.0

SHELF LIFE: INDEFINITE

STORAGE: STORE UPRIGHT IN A
COOL DARK AREA.

CHARACTERISTICS: COLOURLESS, ORANGE FLAVOURED LIQUEUR.

****

COCONUT RUM

COUNTRY OF ORIGIN: CANADA

ALCOHOL %: 28.0 - 30.0

SHELF LIFE: INDEFINITE

STORAGE: STORE UPRIGHT IN A
COOL DARK AREA.

CHARACTERISTICS: A BLEND OF NEUTRAL SPIRIT, COCONUT FLAVOURS,
SUGAR AND RUM.

CREME DE BANANES

COUNTRY OF ORIGIN: HOLLAND

ALCOHOL %: 24.0

SHELF LIFE: INDEFINITE

STORAGE: STORE UPRIGHT IN A
COOL DARK AREA.

CHARACTERISTICS: BRIGHT, CLEAR-YELLOW WITH A STRONG
BOUQUET OF BANANAS.

****

CREME DE CACAO

COUNTRY OF ORIGIN: CANADA

ALCOHOL %: 25.0

SHELF LIFE: 2 YEARS

STORAGE: STORE UPRIGHT IN A
COOL DARK AREA.

CHARACTERISTICS: CHOCOLATE FLAVOUR.

CREME DE MENTHE

COUNTRY OF ORIGIN: CANADA

ALCOHOL %: 25.0

SHELF LIFE: INDEFINITE

STORAGE: STORE UPRIGHT IN A
COOL DARK AREA.

CHARACTERISTICS: MINT FLAVOURED CHARACTERISTICS. AVAILABLE EITHER
COLOURLESS OR GREEN COLOURED.

****

DRAMBUIE

COUNTRY OF ORIGIN: SCOTLAND

ALCOHOL %: 40.0

SHELF LIFE: INDEFINITE

STORAGE: STORE UPRIGHT IN A
COOL DARK AREA.

CHARACTERISTICS: FLAVOUR CAN ONLY BE DESCRIBED AS UNIQUELY DRAMBUIE.

DUBONNET

COUNTRY OF ORIGIN: FRANCE

ALCOHOL %: 18.0

SHELF LIFE: 3-4 MONTHS

STORAGE: STORE UPRIGHT IN A
COOL DARK AREA.

CHARACTERISTICS: A FRENCH AROMATIZED APERITIF WINE WITH A BITTER
SWEET QUININE TASTE.

****

ESPANOLA SPANISH

COUNTRY OF ORIGIN: CANADA

ALCOHOL %: 28.0

SHELF LIFE: INDEFINITE

STORAGE: STORE UPRIGHT IN A
COOL DARK AREA.

CHARACTERISTICS: A BLEND OF COFFEE AND ORANGE FLAVOURS WITH BRANDY
AND NEUTRAL SPIRIT.

FRANGELICO

COUNTRY OF ORIGIN: ITALY   SHELF LIFE: 5 – 7 YEARS

ALCOHOL %: 28.0   STORAGE: STORE UPRIGHT IN A
                                            COOL DARK AREA.

CHARACTERISTICS: GOLDEN YELLOW COLOUR, PREVALENT HAZELNUT TASTE.

****

GALLIANO

COUNTRY OF ORIGIN: ITALY   SHELF LIFE: 2 – 3 YEARS

ALCOHOL %: 35.0   STORAGE: STORE UPRIGHT IN A
                                            COOL DARK AREA.

CHARACTERISTICS: GALLIANO IS A SECRET COMBINATION OF MORE THAN 30 HERBS
                  AND FLOWERS WHICH GIVE IT A SUBTLE TASTE.

GLAYVA

COUNTRY OF ORIGIN: UNITED KINGDOM   SHELF LIFE: 3 YEARS

ALCOHOL %: 40.0   STORAGE: STORE UPRIGHT IN A
          COOL DARK AREA.

CHARACTERISTICS: SCOTCH WHISKEY BASED LIQUEUR.

****

GOLDEN PEAR

COUNTRY OF ORIGIN: HUNGARY   SHELF LIFE: INDEFINITE

ALCOHOL %: 30.0   STORAGE: STORE UPRIGHT IN A
          COOL DARK AREA.

CHARACTERISTICS: GOLDEN PEAR FRUITY CHARACTERISTICS FLAVOURED AND
GOLDEN-YELLOW COLOURED SWEET LIQUEUR.

-28-

GRAND CURACAO

COUNTRY OF ORIGIN: CANADA   SHELF LIFE: INDEFINITE

ALCOHOL %: 25.0   STORAGE: STORE UPRIGHT IN A

                                                         COOL DARK AREA.

CHARACTERISTICS: AMBER, ORANGE (CURACAO) FLAVOURED CHARACTERISTICS.

****

GRAND MARNIER

COUNTRY OF ORIGIN: FRANCE   SHELF LIFE: INDEFINITE

ALCOHOL %: 39.8   STORAGE: STORE UPRIGHT IN A

                                                         COOL DARK AREA.

CHARACTERISTICS: LIQUEUR MADE BY DISTILLATION OF WILD ORANGE

                    PEELS WITH THE ADDITION OF COGNAC.

IRISH MIST

COUNTRY OF ORIGIN: IRELAND

ALCOHOL %: 35.0

SHELF LIFE: INDEFINITE

STORAGE: STORE UPRIGHT IN A
COOL DARK AREA.

CHARACTERISTICS: A WHISKEY BASED LIQUEUR, PRODUCED FROM WHISKEY,
HONEY, FLAVOURINGS AND HERBS.

****

JACK DANIELS

COUNTRY OF ORIGIN: U.S.A.

ALCOHOL %: 40.0

SHELF LIFE: INDEFINITE

STORAGE: STORE UPRIGHT IN A
COOL DARK AREA.

CHARACTERISTICS: A TENNESSEE WHISKEY

KAHLUA

COUNTRY OF ORIGIN: MEXICO

ALCOHOL %: 26.5

SHELF LIFE: 2 YEARS

STORAGE: STORE UPRIGHT IN A
COOL DARK AREA.

CHARACTERISTICS: DARK BROWN COLOUR, COFFEE AND VANILLA FLAVOUR.

****

KEMPER'S BARVARIAN CREAM

COUNTRY OF ORIGIN: CANADA

ALCOHOL %: 17.0

SHELF LIFE: 9 MONTHS

STORAGE: REFRIGERATE
AFTER OPENING

CHARACTERISTICS: RICH AND CREAMY WITH A HIGH BUTTERFAT CONTENT, FLAVOURED
WITH CANADIAN WHISKEY, CHOCOLATE AND COCOA FLAVOURS.

LIQUORE D'ORO

COUNTRY OF ORIGIN: CANADA   SHELF LIFE: 1 YEAR

ALCOHOL %: 30.0   STORAGE: STORE UPRIGHT IN A
           COOL DARK AREA.

CHARACTERISTICS: A BLEND OF NATURAL ANISE, LICORICE EXTRACTS,
        SUGAR AND GRAIN SPIRIT.

****

MELON

COUNTRY OF ORIGIN:CANADA   SHELF LIFE: 3 MONTHS

ALCOHOL %: 25.0   STORAGE: STORE UPRIGHT IN A
           COOL DARK AREA.

CHARACTERISTICS: BLEND OF NATURAL MELON FLAVOUR, SUGAR AND GRAIN SPIRITS.

MIDORI MELON

COUNTRY OF ORIGIN: JAPAN

ALCOHOL %: 23.0

SHELF LIFE: 2 YEARS

STORAGE: STORE UPRIGHT IN A
COOL DARK AREA.

CHARACTERISTICS: BRIGHT GREEN IN COLOUR WITH THE FLAVOUR
OF HONEYDEW MELON.

****

NOISETTE

COUNTRY OF ORIGIN: CANADA

ALCOHOL %: 28.0

SHELF LIFE: INDEFINITE

STORAGE: STORE UPRIGHT IN A
COOL DARK AREA.

CHARACTERISTICS: LIGHT BROWN COLOUR WITH A FLAVOUR OF HAZELNUT
AND BRANDY.

NUT AMBROSIA

COUNTRY OF ORIGIN: CANADA

ALCOHOL %: 28.0

SHELF LIFE: INDEFINITE

STORAGE: STORE UPRIGHT IN A
COOL DARK AREA.

CHARACTERISTICS: SWEET, NUTTY LIQUEUR WITH A MILD AFTERTASTE
FROM THE WHISKEY.

****

NUTCRACKER

COUNTRY OF ORIGIN: CANADA

ALCOHOL %: 28.0

SHELF LIFE: INDEFINITE

STORAGE: STORE UPRIGHT IN A
COOL DARK AREA.

CHARACTERISTICS: NUT FLAVOURED LIQUEUR.

O'DARBY DAIRY IRISH CREAM

COUNTRY OF ORIGIN: IRELAND

ALCOHOL %: 17.0

SHELF LIFE: 2 YEARS

STORAGE: REFRIGERATE
                        AFTER OPENING

CHARACTERISTICS: COFFEE-CREAM COLOUR, CHOCOLATE FLAVOUR.

****

OUZO SANS RIVAL

COUNTRY OF ORIGIN: GREECE

ALCOHOL %: 46.0

SHELF LIFE: INDEFINITE

STORAGE: STORE UPRIGHT IN A
                        COOL DARK AREA.

CHARACTERISTICS: A HIGH-PROOF ANISE LIQUEUR.

PARFAIT AMOUR

COUNTRY OF ORIGIN: FRANCE

SHELF LIFE: INDEFINITE

ALCOHOL %: 25.0

STORAGE: STORE UPRIGHT IN A
COOL DARK AREA.

CHARACTERISTICS: MADE BY THE DISTILLATION OF CITRUS FRUITS AND MACERATION
OF PLANTS TO WHICH ARE ADDED ALCOHOL, SUGAR AND WATER.
A VERY OLD TRADITIONAL RECIPE.

****

PEACH BRANDY

COUNTRY OF ORIGIN: CANADA

SHELF LIFE: INDEFINITE

ALCOHOL %: 25.0

STORAGE: STORE UPRIGHT IN A
COOL DARK AREA.

CHARACTERISTICS: PLEASANT SWEET TASTE OF PEACHES AND BRANDY.

PEPPERMINT SCHNAPPS

COUNTRY OF ORIGIN: CANADA

ALCOHOL % 30.0

SHELF LIFE: 2 YEARS

STORAGE: STORE UPRIGHT IN A
          COOL DARK AREA.

CHARACTERISTICS: A COLOURLESS LIQUEUR WITH A DISTINCTIVE MINT FLAVOUR.

****

PERNOD 40.1

COUNTRY OF ORIGIN: FRANCE

ALCOHOL %: 40.1

SHELF LIFE: INDEFINITE

STORAGE: STORE UPRIGHT IN A
          COOL DARK AREA.

CHARACTERISTICS: MADE FROM THE ESSENCE OF BADIANE AND FROM A SPIRIT MADE
          FROM NATURAL HERBS SUCH AS MINT, BALM AND ESSENCE.

PRALINE

COUNTRY OF ORIGIN: CANADA

SHELF LIFE: 3 YEARS

ALCOHOL %: 25.0

STORAGE: STORE UPRIGHT IN A
COOL DARK AREA.

CHARACTERISTICS: AMBER COLOUR WITH A SWEET NUT, BUTTER AND
VANILLA FLAVOUR.

****

ROYAL TARA IRISH CREAM

COUNTRY OF ORIGIN: IRELAND

SHELF LIFE: 1 YEAR

ALCOHOL %: 17.0

STORAGE: REFRIGERATE
AFTER OPENING

CHARACTERISTICS: BASIC IRISH CREAM WITH CHOCOLATE AND NATURAL
ORANGE FLAVOURING.

SAMBUCA

COUNTRY OF ORIGIN: ITALY

ALCOHOL %: 38.0

SHELF LIFE: INDEFINITE

STORAGE: STORE UPRIGHT IN A
COOL DARK AREA.

CHARACTERISTICS: WHITE ANISE FLAVOURED LIQUEUR.

****

SOUTHERN COMFORT

COUNTRY OF ORIGIN: CANADA

ALCOHOL %: 40.0

SHELF LIFE: INDEFINITE

STORAGE: STORE UPRIGHT IN A
COOL DARK AREA.

CHARACTERISTICS: AN AMBER COLOURED LIQUEUR WITH CITRUS AND
OTHER FRUIT FLAVOUR.

STRAWBERRY LIQUEUR

COUNTRY OF ORIGIN: CANADA

ALCOHOL %: 24.0

SHELF LIFE: INDEFINITE

STORAGE: STORE UPRIGHT IN A
COOL DARK AREA.

CHARACTERISTICS: A SWEET DISTINCTIVE STRAWBERRY FLAVOUR.

****

SWISS CHOCOLATE ALMOND

COUNTRY OF ORIGIN: CANADA

ALCOHOL %: 27.0

SHELF LIFE: 2 YEARS

STORAGE: STORE UPRIGHT IN A
COOL DARK AREA.

CHARACTERISTICS: BROWN COLOUR, CHOCOLATE AND ALMOND FLAVOURED.

TAMARIND

COUNTRY OF ORIGIN: CANADA

SHELF LIFE: INDEFINITE

ALCOHOL %: 35.0

STORAGE: STORE UPRIGHT IN A
COOL DARK AREA.

CHARACTERISTICS: A DELICATE TANGY TRIBUTE TO THE PRIZED CURACAO
ORANGES OF THE DUTCH WEST INDIES, BLENDED WITH
FINE, AGED BRANDY.

****

TIA MARIA

COUNTRY OF ORIGIN: JAMAICA

SHELF LIFE: INDEFINITE

ALCOHOL %: 26.5

STORAGE: STORE UPRIGHT IN A
COOL DARK AREA.

CHARACTERISTICS: A DARK BROWN, SWEET COFFEE FLAVOURED LIQUEUR.

TRIPLE SEC

COUNTRY OF ORIGIN: CANADA

ALCOHOL %: 30.0

SHELF LIFE: INDEFINITE

STORAGE: STORE UPRIGHT IN A
COOL DARK AREA.

CHARACTERISTICS: A BLEND OF CURACAO ORANGE EXTRACT, SUGAR
AND GRAIN SPIRIT.

****

YUKON JACK

COUNTRY OF ORIGIN: CANADA

ALCOHOL %: 40.0

SHELF LIFE: 2 YEARS

STORAGE: STORE UPRIGHT IN A
COOL DARK AREA.

CHARACTERISTICS: A PALE STRAW COLOURED LIQUEUR WITH A DISTINCTIVE
CITRUS TASTE IN A WHISKY BASE.

SHOOTERS

THE FOLLOWING RECIPES STATE ONLY THE VARIOUS LIQUEURS USED IN EACH SHOOTER. THE PROPORTIONS OF THE LIQUEURS ARE DETERMINED BY THE NUMBER OF INGREDIENTS USED IN THE RECIPE. IF ONLY TWO INGREDIENTS ARE USED, THEY SHOULD BE POURED $\frac{1}{2}$ oz. OF ONE, $\frac{1}{2}$oz. OF THE OTHER. IF THREE LIQUEURS ARE STATED, ONE THIRD OF EACH SHOULD BE USED. IF FOUR LIQUEURS ARE LISTED, USE ONE FOURTH OF EACH --- AND SO ON.

YOU MAY WISH TO CHANGE THE PROPORTIONS TO SUIT YOUR OWN PERSONAL TASTE.

A.B.C.

AMARETTO
BAILEY'S
COINTREAU

AFTER EIGHT

CREME DE MENTHE
SWISS CHOCOLATE ALMOND
IRISH CREAM

AGENT 99

GRAND MARNIER
PARFAIT AMOUR
ANISETTE

ALTERED STATE

GOLDEN PEAR
IRISH CREAM
KAHLUA

THERE IS A NEW DRINK OUT NOW – " THE DELEGATE".
TWO OF THEM AND YOU'RE SPEAKING FROM THE FLOOR.

ANGEL HIP

BENEDICTINE
IRISH CREAM

ANGEL KISS

KAHLUA
SWISS CHOCOLATE ALMOND
DROP OF IRISH CREAM

ANGEL TIP

CREME DE CACAO
IRISH CREAM
CHERRY ON A PICK

ANGEL WING

CREME DE CACAO
BRANDY
IRISH CREAM

" DRINKING REMOVES WARTS AND PIMPLES. NOT
FROM ME, BUT FROM THOSE I HAVE TO LOOK AT."

JACKIE GLEASON

ATOMIC BOMB

RYE
TEQUILA

AVALANCHE

KAHLUA
CREME DE CACAO
SOUTHERN COMFORT

B - 52

KAHLUA
IRISH CREAM
GRAND MARNIER

B - 53

KAHLUA
IRISH CREAM
TEQUILA

" IT WAS A WOMAN WHO DROVE ME TO DRINK- AND
YOU KNOW, I NEVER EVEN THANKED HER."

W.C. FIELDS

B – 54

KAHLUA
IRISH CREAM
GRAND MARNIER
TEQUILA

B.B.C.

BENEDICTINE
IRISH CREAM
COINTREAU

B.B.G.

BENEDICTINE
BAILEY'S
GRAND MARNIER

BAD STING

GRENADINE
ANISETTE
GRAND MARNIER
TEQUILA

BLURRED VISION ISN'T ALWAYS IMPROVED BY
GLASSES. ESPECIALLY THE REFILLABLE KIND.

BANANA SPLIT

CREME DE BANANES
SWISS CHOCOLATE ALMOND
STRAWBERRY LIQUEUR
TOP WITH WHIPPED CREAM

BLACK CAT

KAHLUA
BRANDY
OUZO

BLACK DEVIL

DARK RUM
CREME DE MENTHE

BLACK JACK

KAHLUA
ANISETTE

" SOPHISTICATION IS THE ART OF GETTING
DRUNK WITH THE RIGHT PEOPLE."

WALTER WINCHELL

BLOW JOB

KAHLUA

IRISH CREAM

CREME DE BANANES

WHIPPED CREAM

THE SKILLED TECHNIQUE OF A BLOW JOB LIES NOT IN THE MIXING BUT IN THE WAY IN WHICH YOU DRINK IT. PLACING YOUR HANDS BEHIND YOUR BACK, WRAP YOUR LIPS OVER THE RIM OF THE GLASS, THROW YOUR HEAD BACK AND START GULPING. WHEN YOU'VE EMPTIED THE CONTENTS PLACE THE GLASS BACK ON THE TABLE. REMEMBER – NO HANDS!

BULL SHOOT

KAHLUA

WHITE RUM

TEQUILA

BREAK

KAHLUA

CREME DE BANANES

ANISETTE

ANNIVERSARIES ARE LIKE SHOOTERS: AFTER A FEW
YOU DON'T BOTHER TO COUNT THEM.

CANDY CANE

GRENADINE
CREME DE MENTHE
PEPPERMINT SCHNAPPS

CHANNEL 64

CREME DE BANANES
IRISH CREAM
ADVOCAAT

CHOCOLATE CHIP

SWISS CHOCOLATE ALMOND
PEPPERMINT SCHNAPPS
IRISH CREAM

DEEP THROAT

KAHLUA
GRAND MARNIER
WHIPPED CREAM

" WE HAD PROBLEMS RIGHT FROM THE START. ON
OUR WEDDING NIGHT , MY WIFE SAID WE WERE
SEEING TOO MUCH OF EACH OTHER."

RODNEY DANGERFIELD

DEPTH CHARGE

TEQUILA
CHARTREUSE
PINEAPPLE JUICE

DOUBLE JACK

YUKON JACK
JACK DANIELS

EDMONTON OILER

GOLDEN PEAR
BLUE CURACAO

EH – BOMB

TEQUILA
CREME DE MENTHE
OUZO
IRISH CREAM
KNOCK IT BACK AND SAY "EH".

" I KNOW MY CAPACITY FOR DRINKING, BUT
I KEEP GETTING DRUNK BEFORE I REACH IT."

GEORGE GOBEL

ELECTRIC BANANA

TEQUILA
CREME DE BANANES
LIME JUICE

EL REVOLTO

PEPPERMINT SCHNAPPS
IRISH CREAM
COINTREAU

ESKIMO GREEN & GOLD

CREME DE MENTHE
GOLDEN PEAR

401

KAHLUA
CREME DE BANANES
IRISH CREAM
YUKON JACK

THE DOCTORS ARE SAYING THAT DRINKING IS BAD FOR US.
I DON'T KNOW. YOU SEE A LOT MORE OLD DRUNKS THAN
OLD DOCTORS.

FACE OFF

GRENADINE
CREME DE MENTHE
PARFAIT AMOUR
SAMBUCA

FIRE & ICE

TEQUILA
CREME DE MENTHE

FLAME THROWER

CREME DE CACAO
B & B

FLAMING DIAMOND

STRAWBERRY LIQUEUR
PEPPERMINT SCHNAPPS
GRAND MARNIER

" MY NEIGHBOR SAYS HIS DRINKING HABITS DON'T
AGREE WITH HIS LOVE LIFE. HIS GIRL SAYS SHE
WON'T MARRY HIM WHEN HE'S DRUNK AND HE
WON'T MARRY HER WHEN HE'S SOBER."

JOEY ADAMS

FLAMING ORGY

GRENADINE
CREME DE MENTHE
BRANDY
TEQUILA

GHETTO BLASTER

KAHLUA
METAXA
TEQUILA
RYE

GODFATHER

AMARETTO
SCOTCH

GOLD RUSH

SWISS CHOCOLATE ALMOND
VODKA
YUKON JACK

" I WON'T SAY DEAN MARTIN HAS A DRINKING
   PROBLEM, BUT HIS MAIN CONCERN IN LIFE IS
   WHAT WINE GOES WITH WHISKEY."

                              JOEY ADAMS

GRAND BAILEY'S

BAILEY'S
GRAND MARNIER

GRAND SLAM

CREME DE BANANES
IRISH CREAM
GRAND MARNIER

GREAT WHITE NORTH

KAHLUA
IRISH CREAM
ANISETTE

GREEN LIZARD

TEQUILA
CHARTREUSE
TRIPLE SEC

MIDDLE - AGE IS WHEN THE PHONE RINGS ON A SATURDAY NIGHT AND YOU HOPE IT'S THE WRONG NUMBER.

HARD ON

KAHLUA
AMARETTO
IRISH CREAM

HEAVENLY BODY

GOLDEN PEAR
FRANGELICO
IRISH CREAM

HORNEY BULL

VODKA
RUM
TEQUILA

HURRICANE

ANISETTE
BLUE CURACAO
TEQUILA
IRISH CREAM

MOST PEOPLE HAVE NO RESPECT FOR
AGE UNLESS IT'S BOTTLED

IRISH MONKEY

IRISH CREAM
CREME DE BANANES

ITALIAN STALLION

PEPPERMINT SCHNAPPS
SAMBUCA

JELLY BEAN

GRENADINE
ANISETTE
TEQUILA

KAMIKAZE

TRIPLE SEC
VODKA
SQUEEZE OF LIME

" WHEN YOU CAN'T STAND THE TERRIBLE
CRASHING OF SNOWFLAKES AS THEY HIT
THE GROUND, YOU HAVE HAD ENOUGH."

GERALD BARZAN

LANDSLIDER

IRISH CREAM
GRAND MARNIER
AMARETTO

LAZER BEAM

GALLIANO
TEQUILA

LEATHER & LACE

KAHLUA
PEPPERMINT SCHNAPPS
IRISH CREAM

LIGHT HOUSE

KAHLUA
GRAND MARNIER
TEQUILA

" I ARRIVE VERY LATE AT WORK IN THE MORNING
BUT I MAKE UP FOR IT BY LEAVING VERY EARLY
IN THE AFTERNOON."

CHARLES LAMB

LONESTAR

PARFAIT AMOUR
CHERRY WHISKY
RUM

MEXICAN BERRY

KAHLUA
STRAWBERRY LIQUEUR
TEQUILA

MEXICAN FLAG

GRENADINE
CREME DE MENTHE
TEQUILA

MEXICAN PUMPER

GRENADINE
KAHLUA
TEQUILA

A DRINKING MAN'S DIET - IN ONLY THREE WEEKS YOU
CAN LOSE 21 DAYS AND YOUR JOB.

MILES OF SMILES

AMARETTO
PEPPERMINT SCHNAPPS
RYE

MILKY WAY

SWISS CHOCOLATE ALMOND
IRISH CREAM
FRANGELICO

MODEL "T"

KAHLUA
CREME DE BANANES
SWISS CHOCOLATE ALMOND

MONKEY'S PUNCH

KAHLUA
CREME DE MENTHE
IRISH CREAM

" DON'T KNOCK THE WEATHER: NINE-TENTHS OF THE
PEOPLE COULDN'T START A CONVERSATION IF IT
DIDN'T CHANGE ONCE IN A WHILE."

FRANK MCKINNEY HUBBARD

NEUTRON BOMB

KAHLUA
RUM
TEQUILA
SWISS CHOCOLATE ALMOND

19 - DUKE DRIVE

CHOCOLATE MINT
CHERRY BRANDY
CREME DE BANANES

NUDE BOMB

KAHLUA
AMARETTO
CREME DE BANANES

NUTTY BUDDY

FRANGELICO
SWISS CHOCOLATE ALMOND
PEPPERMINT SCHNAPPS

" DEPEND ON THE RABBIT'S FOOT IF YOU WILL,
BUT, REMEMBER - IT DIDN'T WORK FOR THE
RABBIT. "

E.R. SHAY

PANTY DROPPER

GIN
DUBONNET

OKANAGAN

APRICOT BRANDY
STRAWBERRY LIQUEUR
BLUEBERRY LIQUEUR

PENALTY SHOT

CREME DE MENTHE
TIA MARIA
PEPPERMINT SCHNAPPS

PIPELINE

TEQUILA
VODKA

BACHELOR: " A MAN WHO COMES TO WORK EVERY
MORNING FROM A DIFFERENT DIRECTION."

JOEY ADAMS

POPSICLE

APRICOT BRANDY
VODKA
IRISH CREAM

PRAIRIE FIRE

TEQUILA
TEN DROPS OF TOBASCO

QUICK SILVER

TEQUILA
CREME DE BANANES
PEPPERMINT SCHNAPPS

RAIDER

IRISH CREAM
GRAND MARNIER
COINTREAU

" DURING THE HOT WEATHER I KEEP THE WINDOWS
OF MY CAR CLOSED AND EVERYBODY THINKS THAT
I HAVE GOT AIR CONDITIONING."

BOB MELVIN

RICKEY'S

ANISETTE
PARFAIT AMOUR
COGNAC

ROY HOB SPECIAL

JACK DANIALS
IRISH CREAM
PEPPERMINT SCHNAPPS

RYAN'S RUSH

KAHLUA
IRISH CREAM
WHITE RUM

69

CREME DE BANANES
ANISETTE
IRISH CREAM

" I UNDERSTAND THAT INSANITY IS HEREDITARY –
YOU CAN GET IT FROM YOUR CHILDREN."

BOB NEWHART

SCREAMING LIZARD

TEQUILA
CHARTREUSE

SEDUCTION

FRANGELICO
CREME DE BANANES
IRISH CREAM

SHAMROCK

CREME DE MENTHE
CREME DE CACAO
IRISH CREAM

SHIT KICKER

GRENADINE
CREME DE MENTHE
RYE
TEQUILA

" ACTUALLY, IT ONLY TAKES ONE DRINK TO
GET ME LOADED – I CAN'T RECALL IF IT'S
THE 12th OR THE 13th."

PHIL HARRIS

SILVER THREAD

CREME DE BANANES
PEPPERMINT SCHNAPPS
SWISS CHOCOLATE ALMOND

SMARTIE

GRENADINE
SWISS CHOCOLATE ALMOND
TEQUILA

SNAKE BITE

TEQUILA
PEPPERMINT SCHNAPPS

SNAP SHOT

PEPPERMINT SCHNAPPS
IRISH CREAM

" IF AT FIRST YOU <u>DO</u> SUCCEED –
IT'S PROBABLY YOUR FATHER'S BUSINESS."

RED BUTTONS

SOUTHERN BELLE

APRICOT BRANDY
SWISS CHOCOLATE ALMOND
SOUTHERN COMFORT

STOP LIGHT

GRENADINE
CREME DE MENTHE
CREME DE BANANES

STRAWBERRY SHORTCAKE

CREME DE BANANES
STRAWBERRY LIQUEUR
IRISH CREAM

STRAWBERRY KISS

KAHLUA
STRAWBERRY LIQUEUR
IRISH CREAM

" IT'S BETTER TO MARRY FOR MONEY
THAN FOR NO REASON AT ALL."

JOAN RIVERS

SWISS HIKER

SWISS CHOCOLATE ALMOND
CREME DE BANANES
IRISH CREAM

SWISS & WHOOSH

TIA MARIA
FRANGELICO
IRISH CREAM

T.K.O.

KAHLUA
TEQUILA
OUZO

TEQUILA MOCKINGBIRD

SWISS CHOCOLATE ALMOND
AMARETTO
TEQUILA

A MAN USUALLY FEELS BETTER AFTER A FEW WINKS,
ESPECIALLY IF SHE WINKS BACK.

TEQUILA SMASH

TEQUILA
7 - UP

PLACE YOUR HAND OVER THE TOP OF THE GLASS AND THEN BANG THE GLASS DOWN ON THE TABLE. WHEN THE 7 - UP BEGINS TO FIZZ SHOOT BACK THE TEQUILA SMASH.

TETANUS SHOT

DRAMBUIE
RYE

TEST TUBE BABY

GRAND MARNIER
ANISETTE
DROP OF IRISH CREAM

" R.S.V.P. " –

REMEMBER SEND VEDDING PRESENT.

TEXAS CHAINSAW MURDERER

STRAWBERRY LIQUEUR
VODKA

TWISTER

SOUTHERN COMFORT
TEQUILA
VODKA

UPSIDE DOWN MARGARITA

USE TWO SHOOTER GLASSES

#1   3/4 TEQUILA   #2   LIME JUICE   WITH YOUR BACK FACING THE BAR –
       1/4 TRIPLE SEC   LAY YOUR HEAD BACK ON THE COUNTER.
                                                                      PLACE A TOWEL ON YOUR CHEST AND HAVE
THE BARTENDER POUR THE TWO SHOOTERS INTO YOUR MOUTH. STAND UP AND SWALLOW
AT THE SAME TIME. THIS ONE IS GUARANTEED TO MAKE YOU SMILE.

" DON'T MARRY FOR MONEY –
YOU CAN BORROW IT CHEAPER."

GABE KAPLAN

V – 2 SCHNIDER

KAHLUA
IRISH CREAM
FRANGELICO

VENOM

YUKON JACK
SQUEEZE OF LIME

VIBRATOR

IRISH CREAM
SOUTHERN COMFORT

VOLCANO

KAHLUA
OUZO
WHITE RUM

SOME MEN ARE ATTRACTED BY A GIRLS MIND.

OTHERS ARE ATTRACTED BY WHAT SHE DOESN'T MIND.

WAM BAS

SOUTHERN COMFORT
SCOTCH

WARM PUKE

CREME DE BANANES
IRISH CREAM
COCONUT LIQUEUR

ZIPPER

TEQUILA
IRISH CREAM
GRAND MARNIER

ZUC

CREME DE MENTHE
KAHLUA
IRISH CREAM
GRAND MARNIER

I USE TO HAVE A DRINKING PROBLEM –
BUT NOT ANY MORE, NOW I LIKE THE STUFF.

THE DAY AFTER

THE HANGOVER - AS DESCRIBED BY WEBSTERS DICTIONARY IS: " A SURVIVAL. NAUSEA, HEADACHE ETC. FROM DRINKING MUCH ALCOHOLIC LIQUOR." PERHAPS A MORE SUITABLE DEFINITION WOULD BE " THE MOANING AFTER THE NIGHT BEFORE" OR BETTER YET " THE WRATH OF GRAPES."

NO MATTER HOW YOU PHRASE IT, YOU ARE STILL GOING TO FEEL THE PITS AND THERE IS NOT A THING THAT WILL MAKE YOU FEEL BETTER. YOUR FRIENDS WILL BECOME HANGOVER EXPERTS AND TAKING ADVANTAGE OF YOUR WEAKENED CON-DITION, WILL HAVE YOU SWALLOWING EVERY REMEDY EVER TRIED.

THE TRUTH OF IT IS THAT YOUR STOMACH, IN IT'S SEMI-PARALYZED STATE, IS IN NO MOOD TO TRY ANY OF THE LATEST INVENTIONS. THE BEST THING TO DO IS TO LET THE POOR THING REST IN PEACE UNTIL IT HAS THE CHANCE TO COME BACK TO LIFE.

NO MATTER HOW MANY TIMES WE HAVE SUFFERED EACH OF US HAS TAKEN AN OATH TO NEVER TOUCH ANOTHER DROP AGAIN. HOWEVER, THE DESIRE TO RELAX, SOCIALIZE AND HAVE A GOOD TIME SOON MAKES US FORGET OUR PLEDGE AND ONCE AGAIN WE INDULGE IN THE PLEASURE OF DRINK.

ONE INEBRIATE ASKED A POLICE OFFICER

" WHERE AM I?"

" YOU'RE ON THE CORNER OF BROADWAY

  AND 42nd." SAID THE MAN IN BLUE.

" CUT OUT THE DETAILS", SAID THE DRUNK

" WHAT TOWN AM I IN ?"

BEWARE!

I HAD TWELVE BOTTLES OF LIQUEURS IN THE HOUSE AND MY WIFE TOLD ME TO EMPTY THEIR CONTENTS DOWN THE SINK, OR ELSE.

SO, I PROCEEDED WITH THE UNPLEASANT TASK. I WITHDREW THE CORK FROM THE FIRST BOTTLE AND POURED THE CONTENTS DOWN THE SINK, WITH THE EXCEPTION OF ONE GLASS, WHICH I DRANK. I WITHDREW THE CORK FROM THE SECOND BOTTLE AND DID LIKEWISE, WITH THE EXCEPTION OF ONE GLASS, WHICH I DRANK. I WITHDREW THE CORK FROM THE THIRD BOTTLE, AND POURED THE LIQUEUR DOWN THE SINK, WITH THE EXCEP-TION OF ONE GLASS, WHICH I DRANK.

I PULLED THE CORK FROM THE FOURTH SINK AND POURED THE BOTTLE DOWN THE GLASS, WHICH I DRANK. I PULLED THE BOTTLE FROM THE CORK OF THE NEXT AND DRANK THE SINK OUT OF IT, AND THREW THE REST DOWN THE GLASS. I TOOK THE SINK OUT OF THE GLASS BOTTLE THE DRINK AND DRANK THE POUR.

WHEN I HAD EVERYTHING EMPTIED, I STEADIED THE HOUSE WITH ONE HAND, AND WITH THE OTHER FOUR HANDS I COUNTED THE BOTTLES, CORKS, GLASSES AND SINK, AND AS THE HOUSE CAME BY I COUNTED THEM AGAIN. I FINALLY HAD ALL THE HOUSES IN

ONE BOTTLE, WHICH I DRANK.

I'M NOT HALF SO THINK AS YOU MIGHT DRUNK, BUT I FOOL MY FEELISH THAT THE DRUNKER I STAND HERE THE LONGER I GET.